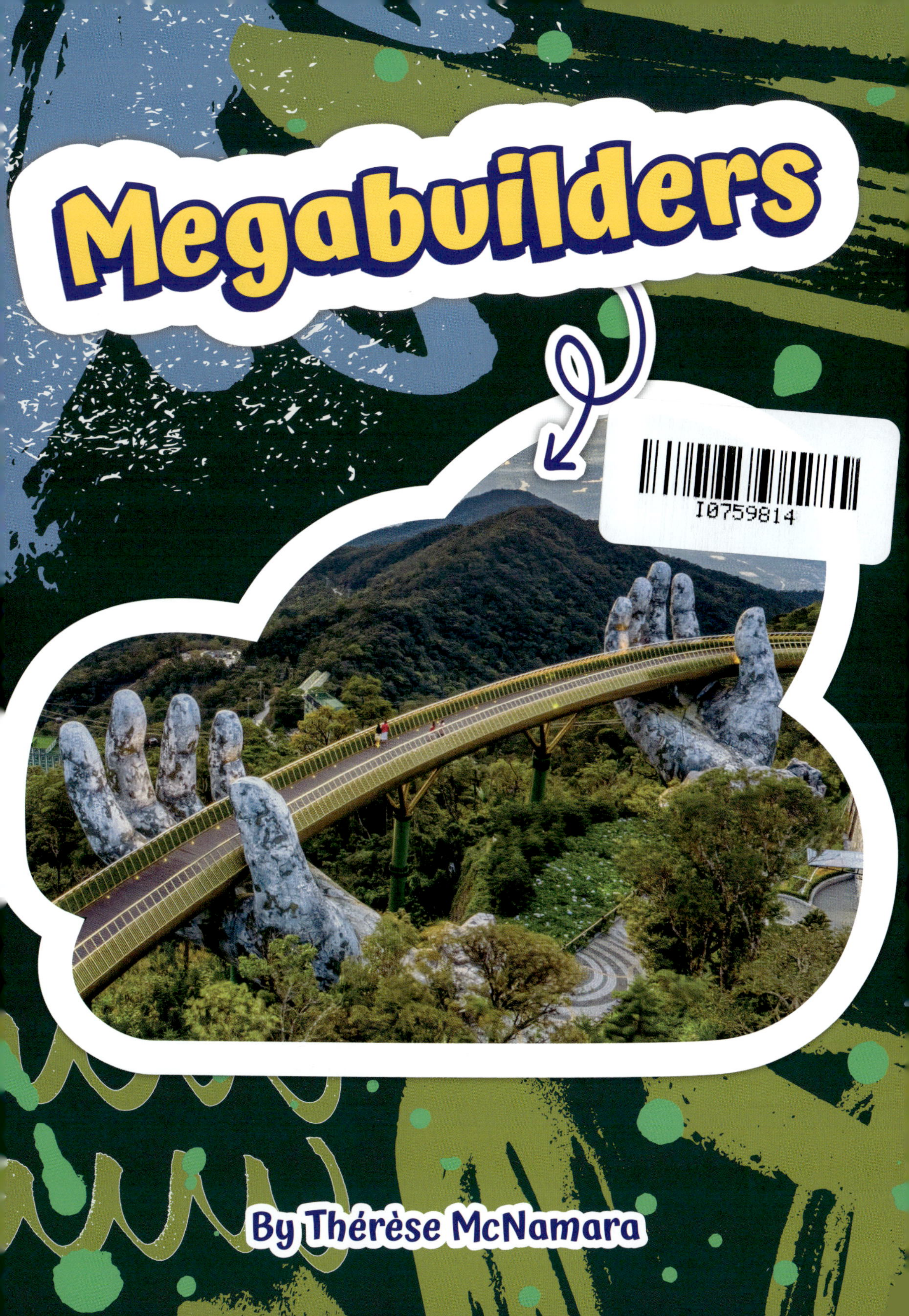
Megabuilders
I0759814
By Thérèse McNamara

The Child's World
childsworld.com

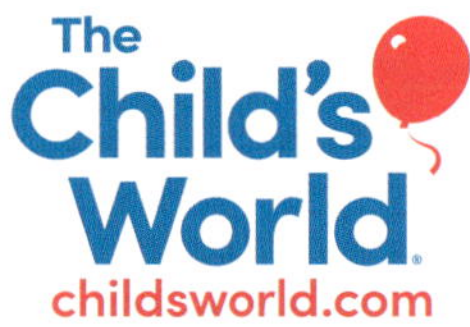

Published by The Child's World®
800-599-READ • childsworld.com

Photography Credits
Hien Phung Thu/Shutterstock.com, cover, title page, 16-17, 29 (top right); David R. Frazier Photolibrary Inc./Alamy.com, 5; travelwild/Shutterstock.com, 6-7; Mariangela Cruz/Shutterstock.com, 8-9; Yuri Yavnik/Shutterstock.com, 10-11, 29 (top left), 30-31; Boris Stroujko/Shutterstock.com, 12-13; Lucy Clark/Dreamstime.com, 13; mbrand85/Shutterstock.com, 14-15; Duc Huy Nguyen/Shutterstock.com, 19; guentermanaus/Shutterstock.com, 20; Nigel Jarvis/Shutterstock.com, 21; Ykartsova/Dreamstime.com, 22; Bob C/Shutterstock.com, 23, 29 (bottom left); Sakis Lazarides/Shutterstock.com, 25, 29 (bottom right); Pong Wira/Shutterstock.com, 27; MinBaMyaing/Shutterstock.com, 28

ISBN Information
9781503877924 (Reinforced Library Binding)
9781503878525 (Portable Document Format)
9781503879065 (Online Multi-user eBook)
9781503879607 (Electronic Publication)

LCCN
2025938215

Printed in the United States of America

Bringing the World to Young Readers 1968

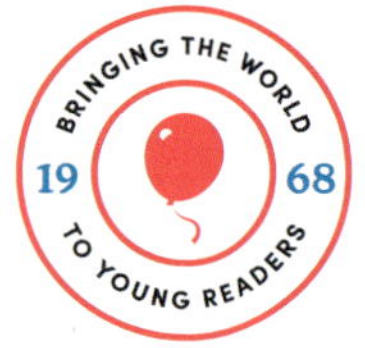

ABOUT THE AUTHOR

Thérèse McNamara was a teacher, a consultant, and then a school administrator. She is now retired and likes to spend time hanging out with her son, playing with her silly poodles, and riding her horses. During quiet moments, she reads mysteries, knits, spins yarn, and gardens. She enjoys traveling to places with waterfalls, castles, ocean cliffs, and mystical mountains.

Table of Contents

AS YOU READ, LOOK FOR OTHER VOWEL TEAMS

CHAPTER 1

Amazing Structures, Far and Wide

Our world is filled with fascinating **structures**. Think about some structures you may have already seen where you live. Or perhaps when you have traveled with your family. Were they tall or short? Simple or elaborate? Old or new?

Some interesting constructions have been built by humans. But there are many others that have been made by nature, either by **flora** or even **fauna**. We may see these creations in our daily lives and not even notice them. There might be a collection of captivating shapes in your very own backyard!

In this book, we'll look at just a few of the world's most fascinating structures. As you read, you will travel to faraway countries. You'll see things that have been built in the sky, on the land, and in the sea. Think about which structures you would like to explore someday. Or maybe you will recognize some that you already have!

DID YOU KNOW?

The Atomium is one of the tallest structures in Belgium. There is an elevator in the center of the building. The steel tubes contain escalators. Inside the balloon-like globes are a restaurant, art **exhibits**, and cultural events. Visitors can look out over the city from a large viewing area, too. *Megacool!*

The Atomium in Belgium is a popular tourist destination.

CHAPTER 2

Ancient Structures

PETRA

In the desert of southern Jordan lies Petra, which is one of the oldest cities in the world. It is a fascinating place that was built around the 3rd century BC. Why is it so interesting? Because all its buildings were carved from stone! *Megasculpting!* Buildings like Al-Khazneh (al-KAZ-neh), also known as "The Treasury," were chiseled into red sandstone cliffs. Al-Khazneh is a large **tomb** that was used for an important pharaoh, or king.

But builders of that time didn't only carve buildings. They also carved statues, roads, walkways, and stairways, along with water grooves, channels, and pools. The city was equipped with a complex water network. This meant that the citizens of Petra had water year-round for food, drink, and bathing.

At one time, as many as 30,000 people lived in Petra. The city was huge, sprawling across 100 square miles (259 square kilometers)! Although only a few desert-**dwellers** live there today, many **archeologists** and tourists still flock to the area. It is truly a jewel of the desert.

DID YOU KNOW?
Al-Khazneh has been used as a location for many Hollywood movies like *Indiana Jones and the Last Crusade*. It has also been shown in video games such as *Assassin's Creed*.

Al-Khazneh, in the ancient city of Petra, Jordan, is a famous landmark.

STONEHENGE

Stonehenge, in Wiltshire, England, is a prehistoric stone monument. No one really knows why it was built. But archeologists think it might have once been a sacred temple. Others think it might have been used as an observatory. Why? The stones are aligned with the movements of the Sun and the Moon. On the morning of the summer equinox, people would gather to celebrate. They watched the rays from the Sun shine directly into the center of the henge.

Stonehenge was built between 3000 and 1520 BC. The stones in the circle are megahuge! Each of the outer stones is around 13 feet (almost four meters) high and seven feet (two meters) wide. A henge stone can weigh up to 25 tons (25,000 kilograms)! Some of the stones were brought from up to 150 miles (241 kilometers) away. How did they do it without any machines or advanced tools? Workers probably placed the heavy stones on sledges. Then they would have rolled them over logs to make them move more easily. It must have been grueling work!

Stonehenge is mega-old!

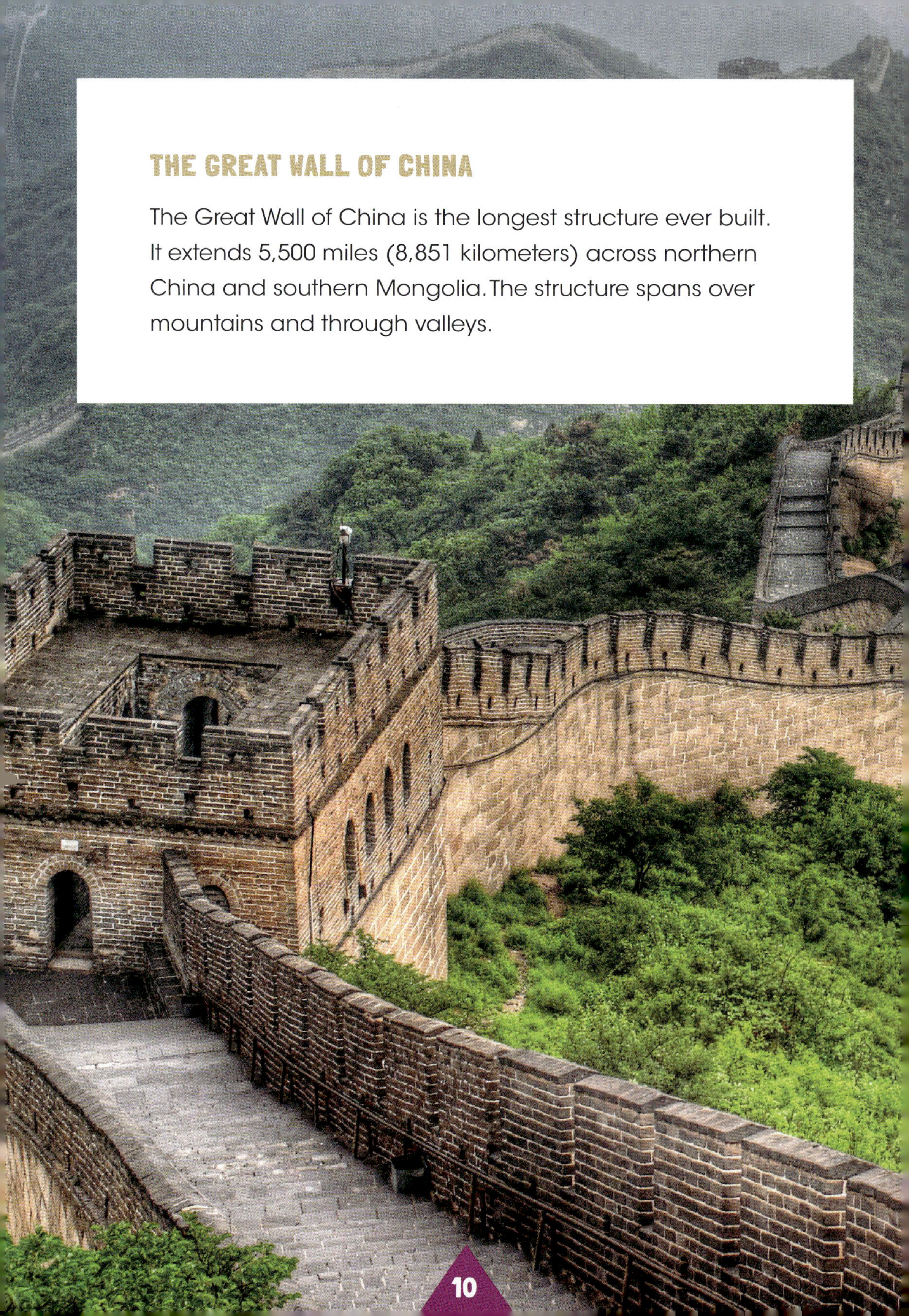

THE GREAT WALL OF CHINA

The Great Wall of China is the longest structure ever built. It extends 5,500 miles (8,851 kilometers) across northern China and southern Mongolia. The structure spans over mountains and through valleys.

The Great Wall was built from tamped-down earth, wood, and bricks. It is, on average, about 30 feet (nine meters) wide and about 16 feet (almost five meters) high. But some sections are up to 50 feet (15 meters) wide!

Early construction started in the 7th century BC. But it took over 2,300 years to complete! *Megalong!* Some parts of the wall are now in ruins. Other large sections remain well-preserved and open to visitors.

The wall served to protect Chinese states and empires from invasions by their enemies. It also helped to keep merchants safe as they traveled along trade routes like the Silk Road. The Silk Road was a collection of trade routes that ran from China to the Mediterranean Sea. Merchants traded silk, tea, and spices from China for things like metals and glassware from the West.

The Great Wall of China is one of the Seven Wonders of the World.

NEUSCHWANSTEIN CASTLE

Neuschwanstein (noy-SHVAN-styn) Castle, in Bavaria, Germany, is not very tall—only 213 feet (64 meters). But it looks megabig because of its location! The gray-colored walls and elegant blue **turrets** make it look like a fairytale castle.

As compared to other castles in Europe, Neuschwanstein is not very old. Its construction was started in 1868 by King Ludwig II. He was known as "Mad King Ludwig" because he wasn't very interested in his kingly duties. Instead, he spent his time in pursuit of other things, like castle building, the arts, and music.

King Ludwig II enjoyed the comforts of the latest technology of the time. His castle had running water, flushing toilets, telephones, and even a central heating system. There was also an elevator from the kitchen to the dining room!

How did workers get the building materials up the mountain? They used a steam crane and **scaffolding**. The king moved into his new castle before it was finished. In fact, the castle was never finished according to King Ludwig II's original plans. It was supposed to have more than 200 rooms, but only 15 were completed before his death. King Ludwig II only lived in the castle for 172 days!

Neuschwanstein Castle in Bavaria, Germany, was built atop a rugged hill.

Neuschwanstein Castle was the inspiration for Disneyland's Sleeping Beauty Castle!

THE TIGER'S NEST MONASTERY

High in the mountains of Bhutan sits a very special place called the Tiger's Nest **Monastery**. A legend tells of a master monk who flew there on the back of a tigress. He stayed and meditated for three years in the caves of these mountains. This site became a holy place for Buddhists. In 1692, monks built the Tiger's Nest Monastery to honor the master monk.

The Tiger's Nest sits nearly 2,000 feet (609 meters) up from the valley below. There is no road to get to it. Instead, travelers reach the monastery by hiking or riding a mule. The long dirt trail up the mountain can be steep in some places. Along the hike, visitors will see many prayer flags, temples, a large waterfall, and a bridge.

The monastery is more than 9,000 feet (2,743 meters) above sea level. *Megahigh!* It is made up of four temples and residences where the monks live. Visitors can wander up wooden bridges and stairs carved into the mountain. They can stroll across balconies to look out over the mountains. *Megabeautiful!*

The Tiger's Nest Monastery is wedged into the side of a lofty cliff.

CHAPTER 4

Brilliant Bridges

THE GOLDEN BRIDGE

The famous Golden Bridge is part of a theme park in the Ba Na Hills of Vietnam. It is also known as Giant Hand Bridge. Do you know why? The structure looks like two large hands holding up a gold-colored bridge. This bridge does not cross over any body of water like most bridges do. Instead, it spans across a mountain and is curved like a rainbow.

The Golden Bridge can be reached only by cable car. Only pedestrians are allowed on this huge structure. It is 490 feet (149 meters) long and about 16 feet (almost five meters) wide. The builders placed beautiful flower beds along each side.

This amazing structure is made of wood, reinforced concrete, and gold-plated steel pipes and railings. The hands look like they were carved from stone, but they are made from steel mesh and **fiberglass**.

The Golden Bridge has had many visitors since it opened in 2018. What do you think people do when they get there? Take selfies, of course! They stand smiling in front of the beautiful bridge and mountains. In the mornings, the bridge is often covered in fog. *Mega-eerie!*

The Golden Bridge in Vietnam was made for people to feel like they were walking on a thread stretched through God's hands.

THE ZHANGJIAJIE GLASS BRIDGE

The Zhangjiajie (zhang-ZHA-zheh) Glass Bridge in Hunan, China, is the world's longest and highest glass bridge. It is **suspended** 984 feet (almost 300 meters) above ground. The bridge spans 1,410 feet (429 meters) in length and 20 feet (six meters) in width. Visitors are invited to walk across huge glass panels. They can look below to the canyon, forest, waterfalls, and streams.

This special bridge can hold up to 800 people at one time! *Megasolid!* There is a metal frame fastened to four large support pillars. The bridge is made with 120 glass panels that are layered solid and without a flaw. Fifty glass balls have been affixed to the surface. Each of the balls weighs about 1,100 pounds (498 kilograms). These balls help to reduce vibrations on the bridge and to keep it stable.

If travelers don't find this unusual bridge exciting enough, there's something else they can try. Bungee jumping! Jumpers can launch themselves from a bridge platform into the gorge 853 feet (almost 260 meters) below. Yikes! *Megascary!* Tourists can also hike on the canyon trails, zip line across the gorge, or take a boat ride along a river.

Rules for visiting the Zhangjiajie Glass Bridge:

1. Visitors must wear shoe covers to keep the glass path clean.
2. Visitors can bring only a cell phone and small-sized bags. Nothing big or heavy is permitted.

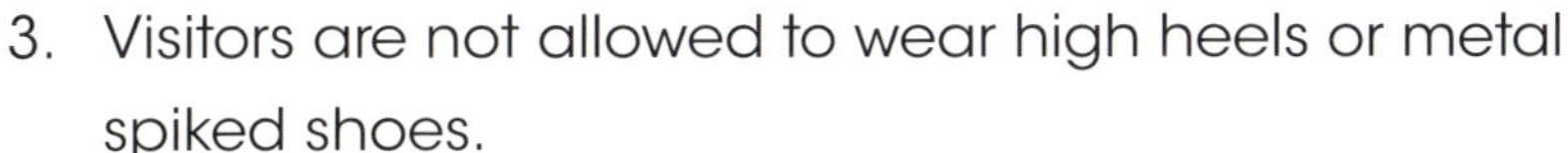

3. Visitors are not allowed to wear high heels or metal spiked shoes.
4. Visitors are not allowed to run or jump on the bridge or stand against the rail.
5. In bad weather, the bridge may be closed for safety.

The Zhangjiajie Glass Bridge in Hunan, China, is one of the most spectacular bridges in the world.

CHAPTER 5 Surprising Plants

THE GIANT WATER LILY PAD

The giant water lily pad grows in the shallow, quieter waters of the Amazon River. It is the world's largest water lily. A megalily! Nature is such an amazing builder!

This plant is well known for its gigantic, saucer-like leaves. They can grow to up to ten feet (three meters) wide! These leaves look pretty on the surface. But watch out! Underneath, they have many ridges and sharp spikes to stop fish and other creatures from eating them. The leaves' ridges trap air below. This helps to keep the large leaves of the plant afloat.

A legend of the Tupi people of Brazil tells the story of a young girl who loved the Moon and stars very much. She even dreamed of turning into one of them. One day, the girl leaned over the water and reached out to hold the Moon's reflection. But it disappeared! A goddess saw this happen. She changed the young girl into the flower of the giant water lily so that she would not be lost forever.

Each giant water lily leaf floats so well that it can support the weight of small animals.

DID YOU KNOW?

The stalks and seeds of the giant water lily can be eaten. Would you eat water lily?

The giant water lily pad is also called Victoria Amazonica, in honor of Queen Victoria.

MOSAICULTURE

Sometimes nature gets a little help with building beautiful structures. That's what happens with mosaiculture! Mosaiculture artists create huge living sculptures that look like animals, people, or other shapes. Their work is mega-inspiring and leaves visitors in awe!

These sculptors start by drawing elaborate plans. Then they mould a form made from steel or other materials. Next, they add thousands of flowers, mosses, and other plants to shape their design. The living plants need to be watered, trimmed, and cared for regularly to ensure the artwork lasts for years.

The first mosaiculture competition was held in Montreal, Canada, in 2000. Since then, the idea has really taken off! Countries like Japan, Turkey, China, and the United States all host international mosaiculture competitions. These events provide opportunities for mosaiculture artists to showcase their best sculptures.

Mosaiculture sculptures can be made into all kinds of shapes.

CHAPTER 6

Spiders, Bees, and Fish in the Seas

PUFFERFISH SANDCASTLES

Pufferfish are truly fascinating animals! They live mostly in tropical or warm ocean waters close to the shore. Pufferfish like to swim in more sheltered areas like coral reefs.

What makes pufferfish so interesting? First, when they are scared, they puff up to a huge size! They do this by sucking up lots of water into their stomach.

Second, pufferfish are very, very toxic. They can be deadly to animals or people if consumed. But some people still like to eat this poisonous fish. It must be prepared by a special chef who knows how to completely remove the toxins.

Last, some types of pufferfish make beautiful patterns on the ocean floor. The male pufferfish build patterned nests to attract mates. They construct their nests by flapping their fins to design circular patterns in the sand. Some of these nests are over six feet (nearly two meters) wide! *Mega-art!*

DID YOU KNOW?

One of the characters on the *SpongeBob SquarePants* cartoon is Mrs. Puff. She is the driving teacher who tries to show SpongeBob how to drive. But SpongeBob is a horrible driver. Every time he crashes, Mrs. Puff puffs up!

Pufferfish puff up to a huge size to frighten away predators.

TRAPDOOR SPIDERS

Some people might find spiders gruesome. Others are intrigued by these little animals.

Trapdoor spiders are large spiders that do not spin webs to catch their prey. Instead, they nest in the ground. They dig burrows and construct trapdoors made of earth, plant matter, and silk. These spiders can be found in many places like Japan, Africa, South America, and parts of the United States. They are usually about one inch (over two centimeters) in length but can grow to almost twice that size.

This spider's burrow is about 11 inches (almost 28 centimeters) deep and two inches (five centimeters) wide. As the spider grows, it makes its burrow and trapdoor bigger. If you were to look carefully at the trapdoor, you might see rings where the spider added to its entrance.

It might be hard to see a trapdoor when it is closed. That's because it is well camouflaged. *Megahidden*. The spider likes to wait quietly inside while holding onto the underside of the door with its claws. When prey gets too close, the spider doesn't just crawl. It jumps out the door and catches its meal! Into its powerful jaws it goes! Then the spider vanishes back inside, slamming the door shut.

A trapdoor spider waits under its door.

BEES

Bees are such valuable creatures. They pollinate trees and plants to give us food and flowers. Bees produce delicious honey that we can enjoy with tea or toast. They manufacture beeswax that we can use to make candles. And they are wonderful builders!

Bees construct beehives using wax and propolis that they make themselves. To build a beehive, bees start by spreading a layer of propolis or "bee glue" on the walls. Then, the worker bees make and collect wax. They chew it up until it is soft. Next, they form six-sided wax cells in which to store their food or eggs. Bees maintain a warm temperature inside to look after the health of the bees and to retain the shape of the hive. They place propolis at the entrance of their hive because it acts as a sanitizer to keep it megaclean and thriving.

Bees work busily in a hive.

AMAZING BUILDERS

What a wonderful journey we've taken of megabuilders throughout the world! We have looked at buildings constructed both long ago and in recent decades. We have considered how builders can be people, animals, or plants. And we have explored how each of these structures is made for its own unique purposes.

These special places have provided protection to their people and dwellers. They offer beauty and interest for tourists to visit and enjoy. Some feature amazing **engineering** skills. Others are places of peace and meditation. And some serve to attract a mate or to store food. Now think about the buildings and structures where you live. Why are they there? Who might have built them? Are there interesting plants, animal nests, or buildings in your town or city? Have fun exploring!

OTHER VOWEL TEAM WORD LISTS

aw
awe
claws
crawl
drawing
flaw
jaws
saw
sprawling

au
because
fauna
launch
restaurant
saucer

oo
balloon
book
cartoon
cool
food
grooves
look(ed)(s)
Moon(`s)
pools
room(s)
too
tools

ew
chew
few
flew
jewel
new(er)
viewing
viewpoint

ui
build(er)(ers)(ing)(ings)
built
equinox
equipped
pursuit
quieter
quietly
ruins

ue
blue
glue
grueling
gruesome
intrigued
Queen
statues
unique

GLOSSARY

archeologists (ar-kee-OL-uh-justs): people who study human history and places where humans lived

dwellers (DWEL-urz): people or animals who live in a certain place

engineering (en-juh-NEER-ing): the science of designing and building

exhibits (ek-ZIB-its): public displays of works of art or items of interest

fauna (FAW-nuh): animals of a specific area

fiberglass (FY-bur-glas): a building material made of resin and glass fibers

flora (FLOR-uh): plants of a specific area

monastery (MAA-nuh-steh-ree): a place where monks live and work together

scaffolding (SKAF-ul-ding): a temporary structure set up on the outside of a building during construction or restoration

structures (STRUK-churz): constructions; things that are built

suspended (suh-SPEN-duhd): hanging from something above

tomb (TOOM): a large vault where the dead are buried

turrets (TUR-uhts): small towers on the top of a castle

INDEX